Stars Light: Fifth Volume

Leaf

Volume 1

By Dr. Abol H. Danesh

Trafford PUBLISHING® · www.trafford.com

North America & international
toll-free: 1 888 232 4444 (USA & Canada)
phone: 250 383 6864 ♦ fax: 812 355 4082

Table of Contents

In Defense of the Gullibles

Man's tongue is the machine gun and with masterful access to the bullet amunication dictionary and the right choices of words he can literally turn his audience brain into a sieve en route his ears toward total surrender. Therefore, in order to counter this assault when there are abuses of this deadly arsenal, imagine you are a massive rock and the bullets are the popcorns ...bouncing up and down on you for your entertainment and nothing else after the show is over...

The Horrific Beauty: In human body. There are three places that the savage barbarism and sublime civilization. Meet one another in a joint common ground. His nails. His hairs. And his Teeth. As long as these three barbaric civilization oxymorons know that. All three of them are hosted by soft humane tissues. We might be ...

Beesetoon: Magnificent ceiling. taller than any known palace made by man. Decorated with endless bulbs of light at night. Standing on its own. Without the support of any known standing pillars. As fresh air moves in and out in perfume. This ever high ceiling is the roof of man's only shelter. Build to save him from the demon. That is lurking somewhere in the outer space and beyond.

Deep Minds in Deep Union: It was me and it was me again and the flower. Three of us sat together. We did not utter a word for quite a long while. Until a friend came by. To sit with us to continue the same conversation we had left in triad in utter silence

Stitches: If you think you can stitch the broken heart in the same way you can stitch the broken body, then you need to think again for the former is the work of god without payment and the latter the work of man who must get paid in advance upon showing your insurance card before visitation

Perfume—

Fresh apple unskinned. Is an open jar of perfume. In it still intact the essence of its spring blossom. Upon its conception. As a promising child. But orange! You must cut through its thick skin with bare hand or sharp knife. So it can open up it's sealed off jar of perfume in generosity. Of course with all the mist in expulsion. Orange after the cut. Wish to be treated as an equal to apple. Now that its perfumed water dropping all over the places in plenty—

Best Wishes

Shooting star
High above in heaven
Born in light
Live all the way in light
In Straight path
Then die in light only to disappear

Be happy now:

All the frustration,
disappointment,
dismay
and your great sense of anger
will all vanish and come to an end upon your death
Close your eyes,
inhale and exhale gently
as you step inside the corridor of death in slow motion

January Thaw: **Man is a giant icicle**. And from genuine exercise. Sweat may begin to roll down from his eyebrow to the ground. Like a melting icicle during the January thaw. But dripping is deceiving. For in few short hours. The cold will set in. And with it. Only the icicle man to get a bit thicker and colder. From what he was before the thaw. Staying there like a tall standing statue of Ice in long freezing cold. Yes indeed we all need reliable refrigerator. TO keep us all away from ruins, rotten spoil, bad odor, and corruption.

Wish: The season of fall has arrived in full swing, Trees one after another have become naked without the wings, Their leaves falling down toward earth, Just like the shooting stars but with the sing, But what is it that these shooting stars are singing? Yes, Hassan what do wish now that you are in the ring? My reply to the shooting leaves stars mounted into only one word: The ever green

Untitled: My best written poem is a blank page, showing off to my ancestors, They just can't fool me, With their half baked scribbling on the stone wall in a damp cave, To tell me, they preceded me and they were before me. Yes, you figured it all right, the title of this poem is "Mute"

The greatest Fish on earth: The gentle pristine clean river. Flow slowly & quietly. On a flat shallow floor in earth. It is all transparent. Inside out in a sunny day. And the reflection of its waves on the river bed. Looks like fish scales without end. ...

Body:

Feast of mind has depth like a thick book of poetry,
with table after table of food back and forth all
compressed to one another without gluing... but the
feast of body has only one page and on its backside
there is nothing meaningfully edible found one can
speak of with confidence.

In Memory of Drunken Ahmed

I told him the smell of dry perfumed wood fire is the
greatest of all
In response he smiled
I asked him for the reason behind his mystical smile
as if there was a subliminal message
He smiled again and said the smell of freshly made
food far better

An Illiterate Love Dove

A blank white page
That hasn't been yet poisoned
With the ink of poet
And yet not being raped
By his erected lustful cock pen
Is a clean unscratched window
Opening to the fresh world of spirit
Where a white sweet love dove
Leaves a dark room
For the fresh air of heaven
Without ever looking back

The Unit of Love

A lone petal breaks away from the flower.
Falling...
Not only to announce its independence in loneliness.
But also it's meaning...
A thin leaf in essence.
Yet wrapped in color of love.

The Deadline

A bare stark tree.
With all its naked branches.
Appears as human brain.
But when leaves worn later.
It Becomes a grown up brain.
Then that's brain hard at work on a project with deadline.

The Blank Page—

The Tabula Rasa
It is so sad.
To see man with friends.
With family members.
Who has written or read pages after pages of books,
magazine, newspaper.
Or has given interesting speeches.
But once dead.
They only scribble few words on a flat stone in
piercing in hurry. And then put it on top of him.
To summarize his entire life time journey
achievements
For folks who come visit him to witness
What he has been doing all these years
When he was busy walking on earth

Future

The moment the child is borned.
The best husband is dad.
The best wife is mom.
As mom and dad focus on the future.
The way to hold on to their union.
With it to navigate. Into the unknown.
Into the promising stars filled Milky Way.

Expanding the Frontiers of Kindness

You go to poor,
they speak of injustice and betrayal.
You go to rich and to the super rich they also speak of
injustice and betrayal.
You go to the priest, to the proletariat, to the
bourgeoisie, to the king in his glittering palaces,
they all too speak of injustice and betrayal done to
them.
However the moment you find them dead with red
blood pumping still
Throughout their body,
then you see...

--The Intravenous—

After some miles of running,
The sweat begun running down,
From my eyebrow, To the ground,
In slow motion,
One drop at a time,
Just like the gentle drops of intravenous entering the
patient body in coma.
Upon receiving these drops during my two hours of
ICU hospitalization,
Rolling down from head to toe,
I surely got up from death bed, toward somewhat of a
recovery

A Poem for Remembering—

The blue ocean roars and roars a little more.
 Up and down in wave to keep on pour.
Even it sometimes goes over the board.
To make a little pot hole lake. Like a little core.
The overflow sometimes.
Flows like a river.
That later on come back.
To join the ocean with roar.
Just a little reminder for the vast ocean in gore.
Not to forget its humble beginning.
Like a poor river in bend and bow in soar

Recycling Rum

On the sand beach
With Ocean waves crashing on the shore
lay down an empty large rum bottle
the wind blowing onto the bottle making sounds...
Oh as defender I once held the Rome together intact
But they found a way to get into my sealed head
They finished up the juice of my oath
They drank up the spirit of my resolve
Now I am only an empty shell drifting
Hoping someone to pick me up again
To throw me back in the hell fire of recycling
So at least a tiny piece of me
Could go to make a bottle
With head sealed holding the Rome again in vow

--How to Smoke Science--

Any given ideology.
Is like a hose.
Punctured at different places.
And regardless of which tape or glue to use.
To block the holes.
With increased water pressure.
The hose is bound to leak. More and greater.
Just like a typical ideologue.
Who keeps constantly explaining?
The cropping up of anomalies.
By making up ever more unusual stories.
On the verge of stupidity.

Will Power

I was thrilled once I saw.
My friend had given a rare gift to my daughter on her birthday.
Yes inside a cute red brick size car.
Both radio and CD player had been placed beautifully.
Speakers installed as car front tiers.
Other day spotted a fancy man made wooden Roaster.
Inside of which a cool fan was housed.
For while.
I felt main feature of post modernism.
Was juxtaposition of two different entities.
But Now only will power.

Star Bow—

My bright daizies.
Have exploded in light.
On the top of thin but tall branches.
Like constellation after constellation of stars in the
Milky Way.
But the yesterday heavy rain.
Had been too hard on them during the reign.
Thus some have bent all the way.
To touch the green lawn.
They now are land stars in bow.
While still connected to their roots in the milky way--
A*H*A*D*

--Ruins—

Man should hang a framed picture of run down home
and shack on his wall,
So as he refurbishes, enhances and upgrades his place
of residence, slowly and gradually,
To a respectable clean cut home,
With all the work and labor spent,
Always to remember his roots,
When he looks at that picture once in a while,
To make sure he has not evolved into a rude privileged
exclusionary hood.
Roots! Bottom

The Blood of Messiah on Soil

Man
Spends much of his time
To build himself
Better and greater shelter
All the way until his shelter
Metamorphoses into a glittering mansion
But the irony is
His permanent residence at the end
Ends up being outside of his own beloved residence
--The graveyard--

Eavesdropping

She asked me
To read more books
To improve my vocabulary
To enhance my options for presentation
So my poetry could become
More Dazzling and more attractive
In response I told her
Dear I write poems not for an audience out there
But for myself from within
Like a bubbling musical fountain
Flowing Right inside of a dark hard rocky mountain
And as far as this person is concerned
I enjoy every bit of it
And hope the audience as well
If they choose to put their ears on the mountain
For eavesdropping

To Prolong the Prolonging

Some weeds
Have learned
Over the long course of adoption and survival
To redress themselves
To appear as leaves of flowers
But the thing is
No matter how long the gardener waits for them
They only grow and no news of flowering but
frowning
This is the time that
The uprooting hands of patient gardener
NO longer get fooled
By the camouflaging

Diaper

I
Love
The poem a child writes
While sitting on his parents' lap
Pressing the keys on the computer
In utter randomness in giggles & excitement
Of course...
Once the child's work is done
It is time to print the baby's work
Then print it to hang it from the wall
In a nice expensive frame
To see what heaven was replaying to the baby
In utter classiness while pooping in his diaper
Okay...okay.... I heard you
The parents can help the baby in his art work
By holding and releasing the shift and the cap lock
To improve the quality of art work

Moments: Feeling Impoverished

No matter how many times
You have eaten from open café
Spreading their colorful tasteful tables of food and drinks
Ever farther into the street for great visibility
You feel inferior as if you are from a lower caste
Even if for only once you pass by them
And don't have enough money in your pocket
To eat out in its hustle and bustle of publicity

Surely man is utterly forgetful
When it comes to leisure and good time

Odor & Germ

When see the neighbor
Letting their dog
Come leaving its waste in your backyard
Don't go to them asking:
Mom, Is this your dog
Coming to my backyard ...
Instead ask correctly
Is this you who is coming to my yard keep ...
For when it comes to waste
Are carnivores' waste are the same
And unlike the vegetarians
They all spew bad repulsive odor
Attracting lots of nasty flies spreading germs

Natural Denture

Ever time
I skin a good size ripe mango
To eat it like a savage to the end
When I reach its large hard core
I feel as if I am wearing a bony denture
That has come out
Having hard time to put it back
In order to get back
To the natural feeling of my own teeth
I go ahead skin a kiwi
Eating it all the way to the end
Now I have my denture back in my mouth
As natural as any human being can feel

Inside the Bunker

Strong wind blowing in relay summer...
Large and small trees
All bend and bow in music
And their branches full of green leaves
Move back and forth in an unease awakening in
agitation
Some even break apart to descend
With the season of fall still way far in the background
Nonetheless...
The roots remain in standstill
Unshaken in the deep dark
Holding their ground
Without yielding to the wind
Even for a tiny bit compromise

In Rib

I
Am
That
the
Thy Poor
who lives in
Glorious glittering glory
with the shine outshining
all the shines emanating
from all kings' palaces

Throw Out All Your Astronomy Books All at Once

For your face
Is the full moon
That has just about risen in the east
For Your eyebrows
Are the crescent moon few day old
For your nose
Is the submit of mountain
Connecting to its mountain range cheeks
For your eyes with sparkles in them
Are those bright winking stars
For your ears are the spiral milky way
Of which the earth is only a part
For your open lips in open happy laughter
Are the sun itself in a happy autumn day
For your chin is the little or big dipper
Which of course depends upon
The size of your dimple in it whirlpool power
And of course your forehead
Is the large kindergarten book
That has been opened up in full
Before your star eyes in awe
Do I need to go on further to say
The pen will go to construct which part of your body
Or should I announce class recess right now?

The Ever Lasting Fire in Mid Air

My fence rose
That comes in deep red
Has matured
Well into its graceful old age
With branches
Spreading all over the fences
And I am laying down in lush green grass in late
spring
Watching this mega red fire in hanging
In air in smokeless perfume
Wondering...
When this blazing fire place in suspense
could ever completely extinguish
as some of its fire petals
gently separates, breaks away and descends on earth
in utter softness & humility

Hats Off

What
Better hat
One can put on
Than the hat of education graduation
And then once worn and pictures taken
Begin to throw it all up in air in hurray
To ecology not only the sweet freedom
But also some room for the hat of ignorance
Without which life as we know it
Is inconceivable

The Immaculate Conception: Tic

When
Buying a new house
Make sure the following list is complete
Or else you will become regretfully regretful
For the rest of your life
1. Hard Wood Floor
2. Large Windows
3. Large kitchen with eating areas
4. Spacious dining room for the guests
To show your humanity
5. Large backyard with pristine immaculate lawn
6. A lavish and generous pool for perfection
7. Charming living room to show life matters
8. Food? Ignore it completely to
Save money for exquisite furniture
After you moved in

Questioning...

After I saw
In Michelangelo's painting in Vatican
All the angels
Surrounding the God
In a closely knit communion
And then compared my loneliness
To His most famous lone
I said to myself
This is not God who is all by himself alone
But myself who is far away from the communion of
Both Demons and the angels

Now the question is
What God does with these lovely angelic sweethearts
When all the lights are turned off at night

Fun: Order is Good but...

From order
There comes the intimidation and horror
And of course the more perfection of it
The greater horror it will muster under its belt
Thus if you wish to make friends and more friends
Particularly from the social class of less fortunate
Learn to mix that order of perfection with some sense
of chaos
For as far as order and chaos is concerned
There is no limit to each side of the spectrum

Funny Sparrow

A typical brownish sparrow
Had gone on the top of a tree
With full white & pinkish blossom In a sunny day in
spring
Singing his best song
Ever he could come up with
What is he singing
I have dream...
A day that I could sing as sweet as a finch in love
I have a dream ...
A day that all birds are listen to carefully
I have a dream ...
A day that I could finish my singing journey
Now that I have taken my first step
I have a dream...
To break from my spryness rank and free

The Frowning Face Revisited

Ever time I see a man saying after his meal:
O thanks Lord
I am now all fed
Feed those who are hungry
I tell myself:
O what a lie...
For man's stomach throughout his life time
Is like an endless abyss well
And it will never ever get filled
Even if he has eaten up to the rim
His most delicious lunch or dinner
In row and for few weeks in fine dine

Here it in Persian: We are on the same team

The Europeans
Started and then finished
Two painful world wars
Only to figure
"It" was only all about money stupid
However there are few countries left in Europe
Who still resist
To accept this way too simple and stupid solution
Well...
Let's wait and see
If they can pull off the Rabat
Along with flying love dove
Right out from their cute purse to show off
Their intelligent trick
For overcoming the world conflict
--jaguar yore many--

I Am Reigning Now/

Despite
All the will power
I put in managing
A cluster of grape
During the eating while standing
At least one breaks free from the grip of my dominion
Falling on ground saying:

Remember this
Part of me must become wine
This is my heavenly destiny
That must be fulfilled
Beyond and above your will power

Variety: Expanding on Greek Mythology

Today I spotted
A brownish female sparrow
But with golden head of a finch
Surely a rare breeding
And after some thought and reflection
I told myself
When man cannot find his lover on his own term
His choices for mating is surely limited
Particularly when he is in rush
And has no time
To consider optic for birth control
O well ... who knows
Charles Darwin might have had a different take

Hot House

Remember
No matter
How grand and beautiful one's house is
He must get out of it
For fresh air and spirit
Only available out in public
Or else his splendid house
Becomes an equivalent of hunted run down shack in
shantytown
Filled with the spirit of demon
In entrapment
Now having said that
Improve your place of residence bit by bit
Or move to new location for a new shake up

ID: The Computer Key Board Identity
Virgin

It
Carries
Sixty eight signs
Mounted on forty seven keys
To stress the fact that
In the world of scarce resources
Every bit of saving space
By going vertical
To avoid uncontrolled sprawling
Into the virgin hinterland
Is a great virtue
Worth pursuing
By nails
If not
Tooth

Seagull the Teacher

The river was transparent and cool
The seagull after so much search & navigation
Flew few feet high and then dive
To catch the detected crab under water with the beak
Surprise ...surprise ...
Sat next to me unusually way too close
Only to begin to devour the food
Surprise ... surprise...again ....
The Henry seagull left few small pieces behind
only to fly up in search
to catch more living creature for food
but why did the hungry seagull left
some small pieces behind?
Yes, it is customary when you eat your meal with
company
you don't lick the place to the last fiber
before heading once again
for business to find the food

The Naked Heaven

Sky is the tree
Its tiny leaves are the stars
And they are falling
In acrobatic dancing
In abundance
Like a windy day in atom
With excess leaves up in air flying
And when these wintry bright leaf flakes
Descend on earth
They cover the naked trees
As their heavenly leaf dress in light
To keep her ready in full attire
For the anticipated wedding ceremony
At the expense of
Keeping the heaven tree naked
Stripped of most if not all their star leaves

The One: Long Stem

I took out
My favorite
Dried out
Maple leaf
That I was hiding it for long sleep
Between the pages of
My favorite book
Now I let the sun shine
Touch the leaf on its "edge" straight through
With its shadow now casting
On my favorite book
In a shape identical with its own stem
But quite longer
I put the flattened leaf
Back in its book bed
With all the lights off
Toward its long uninterrupted sleep

Border: Why Abraham Lincoln Was Assassinated

I
Am
Not
Against
Giving
Freedom
Liberty
And pursuit of happiness
To the slaves and to my subservient
As long as in the process
They don't come back
To claim my freedom, liberty
And my pursuit of happiness
Simply said
There should be put in place a mechanism
Before hand
So the liberated won't Push their Luck!

Ground Zero

What kind world we live in?
What kind of world...
It has become all materialistic
Devoid of spirit
and in order to reach the material
Man slit another man's throat
as comfortably as
He cuts cheese for breakfast without thought
yet the unit of this beloved material
On which he builds his aspiration for wealth and more
body
That is right the penny
Is spread like dog drops in street
Yet no body bothers to pick it up
To put it back in his piggy bank
For time of emergency
Then one wonders
Where materialistic folk's ties are
When you don't find them bending
"To pick it up"
Help make their dream come true
With a solid base intact and unshakable

Treasury Department

I
Have hung
A bird feeder from the tree
As small birds poking at the holes for the seeds
For every single seed they devour
They drop several seeds on the ground
To say out loud:
You should be generous to others
By sharing your food to the less fortunate
Particularly when your food itself
Came to you free
Straight from the treasury department

Being a Dead Horse:
Legitimate Brutality Revisited

The Greatest
Folly of modern man
Is to test and retest
Again and again
On the dead man
To find
The bottom line of endurance
From which to build a new recorded standard
A crystal clean "Case"
To apply to common man
As legitimate
As legal
With recorded proof
Achieved in objective experimentation

The Horror of Urban Landscape

An outdated digital camera
I inherited from my daughter
After some play
The camera stopped working altogether
Thus I began to break up the camera
Like a little boy in curiosity
With mud and worm dangling from his mouth
What I found inside the box though was amazing
On its little platform
There was a miniature map of
Miniature Traffic Intersection,
Homes zoning, gas station, business district, etc.
All appeared with small tiny wires in camouflage
With invented dots of melted lead
Juxtaposed to one another so so closed
Indeed it was the map of large megalopolis urban sprawl
Right under my stunned and gazed up eyes and mind
What I left with after the camera break up
Was the idea that who the grand master was?
And who were the workers who put this amazing structure
On the back of a tiny brownish thin slate

The Piano Teeth

Her lovely laugh
In a beautiful sound
In a gentle exhaling
Appeared on a set of
Long and extended white teeth
All in perfect order
Inside her all opened up mouth

At first I thought for the first time
I am looking at the piano keyboard
All in crispy shiny white
With a music identical to human sound
When he is in absolute happiness n jubilee

My Absolute Icicle Wrist Watch

From the tip of long & extended icicle
Drips of diamond
Gently falling on the ground
Under the pleasant warm sun rays
Just like the minute hand of
My wrist watch
Except at uneven interval
Stressing the fact that
The same amount of time
Can be experienced and felt
Differently in duration
Depending upon zillions of things
Happening in the Cosmo
In interaction with one another
Or in standstill

My friends when it comes to find the accurate time
With great precision
Forget the Swiss watch
Instead look for crispy diamond icicle watch
It even works and shows time accurately even when
time itself is frozen

The Illiterate

I
Planted
Several morning glory seeds
In a pot full of nutritious soil
With couple of sticks inserted in there
Now after couple of months passed
In cold winter freeze
When everything is frozen
Except the evergreen trees
Every now and then
I see one or two of them in full bloom
In a surprise delight
Like finding a guest from paradise
Waiting for you from behind the window
In an splendid colorful attire
In green skirts
That spell the word love for the illiterate

Submit at once!

Man
Has gone to moon
Man has invented electricity and computer
Man has made awe braining medical break through
Man has invented TV, Radio, and Telephone
Man has made endless list of impossibilities possible
But has fallen by the way side and miserably
To combat his arch enemy to bring him
under his whim and control
Threatening his very existence on the planet earth
Ladies and Gentlemen it is not the global warming
But surprise...
It is the number of babies he brings to life
when he is involved in
hotly hot affairs in full penetration
in an equally hotly hot bed in utter forgetfulness
of all the rest of human consideration

Hot Soup

It was winter
It was cold
It was windy
It was brutal but beautiful
It was a sunny day
It was covered with snow
I walked for hours
Icicles were hanging from my long mustache
In between
I passed by a house
With the chimney in full swing
The smell of burning wood
Blowing toward me from distance
Was the greatest perfumed
I had ever smelled in my entire life
I was warm ... it was inviting...
I felt right at his home before his fire
yet with all wood smoke perfume intact within
without a bit of it escaping to the outside world
when I reached my home
I felt the spirit of Lord in warmth
had filled the entire space in immaculate silence

Luxury Hotel as Class Room

If
Someone
Has been keep snubbing you
With his house
Take him to a luxury hotel
To snob him back
And if still he has not learned his lesson in humility
Threaten him that
You might next time
Take him to see
The glittering shining palace of the emperor
For after all
Home is made for man for his rest
Regardless how humble
Some of them are constructed

A Little Laugh at the Speed of Light

I
Am
God
All there is in the universe
All reside within me
All galaxies reside within me
Nothing exists outside of me
Time does not exist
Speed does not exist
For they are only man made creations
Sprung up from his primordial self-deficiencies
From which he will never recover
For he needs job and more jobs

Post

When
You see
So many
Baseless, rude, corrupt and arrogant individuals
Have come to fame and honor
In public life
Rest assure that
There are as many great original men of honor
Have been berried in the dungeon
Without letting the world
See their light

Indeed!
Joseph has been thrown in the well
by the insignificant evil doers
In order to beef up their own resume
Indeed!

Slow Motion

There is warm fire power
In the crowd
In the social gathering
In the partying
In the intermingling
And then there is warm fire power
In being alone
In being in silence
In being in isolation
In being in meditation
In being alone thinking
Imagining...Imagination...
And if you are locked in the second category
yet without fire
you then better do something
Even if it means to beg
and spend all your saving money
to join the first category
Or else you will freeze into death in slow motion
in a deep depression

Can They Improvise?

Some folks
In gang society
Speak so self assured
Using only the very extreme tip of their tongue end
To impress others and show their brevity
While keeping the rest of it virtually idle
Except for food swallowing
You wonder what will happen to them
If in an accident
They lose that small tip of their tongue

The Isosceles sand time

From
The sharp edge of icicle
hanging in suspense from the roof
Fresh crispy transparent tiny ball of water
just like a sweet rounded diamond
in slow motion dripping down...
But as it drips
The length of icicle itself increases slowly
Despite the meltdown
Like a sand time box
Except as it tics in drip down
You get more sands
Accumulated in the upper floor of glass time sand box
Wage the need of invasion
To let the sand time flow further in the future

Awaiting For the Total Victory

Infinite whiteness
In form of white snow
With the depth
Enviable by any floating iceberg
This infinite whiteness
Coexists peacefully as equal with
Infinite darkness
For almost six months
In the north pole
Until this coexistence of the two equals
Shifts to the south pole
But I tell you this
With the increasing global warming
At the end
The darkness wins the whiteness
Regardless for how long more
The aurora ornaments the sky of north pole
With its dazzling colors in delightful light

Saddam Hessian Danish

I
Look at the time magazine
I see Brock Abeam
This week
The other week
As the
Man of day
Man of week
Man of month
Man of year
I look at other publication
I find the same pattern
Here and there and every where
As if the entire planet earth
Is vaporized in an all out nuclear blast
And the only survival from this human catastrophe
Is Brock Abeam

Gentlemen let's together damn the world of
journalism and press
Until it will rise from the damnation
In order to hold its principle
Not by the Iraqi journalist shoe
But by the iron running legs of Hessian Danish

I am Saddam Hessian Danish
And willing to negotiate

Take Side Before It's Too Late

There are
Two kinds of running
A man who runs
To kill another man
And a man who runs
To save the life of a man
Just in the same way
The wind blows in the season of fall
To put the trees in sleep
And the same wind blows in the season of spring
To awaken the sleeping trees back to
life
Just in the same way the same rain
Brings death and life
Depending upon in which season
It is pouring...

Ho ... Santa Claus Coming to the Town

The way
Almost all human society is set up
Has the tendency
To turn man's heart into the stone
That is to live in society
Is to become stone heart
For man must interacts to survive
In close ended and close minded rings
But thanks to all the human festivities and celebration
Scattered throughout all the four seasons
Which they all work as shock therapy
To revive the stone heard
From the dead to the living
And to restore his heart once again
Imbued with spirit

Land Stars

The yesterday last night fluffy snow
has descended
from heaven to earth
with it of course
the plenty of stars of sky
have landed also on earth with course
Yeah it is a sunny day now
And you can see endless diamond stars
shining through in day light in snow

The sky with all its stars now behold
can be seen on earth in joy in burst

Revisiting the Second Law of Thermos Dynamics

Lord
has made man
in the same way that
Man has built his own dwelling
specially the tall vertical structure
from work place to his home residence
but...
Without constant repair and right posture
Man will face the same destiny
As his own built structure toward the bending & break
down
No matter how strong his backbone is made
Therefore learn to walk straight & erect
With constant effort & self reminder
As if a doctor has inserted a steel
Inside of you from shoulder to your hip
To help you avoid back pain in an expensive surgery
In order to postpone a little longer
The Inevitable!
The Inevitability!

The Men

Each man
Is a man onto itself
And a man outside of himself
And a man
Who does not listen
To that man
Who is outside of himself
For advise and recommendation
In the waterless barren desert of creativity
Is doomed to rot under sun
And then be buried alive
In the sand storm
As the fresh food supply
For the scorpions

They Defend Nothing worth Fighting For

When
The Get going
gets tough
the tough gets going
and the opportunists and the cowards
go somewhere else
to make more money
until the get going
gets softer & gentler & more civilized
for their return

Meal Time:
the King Arthur's Round Table

A seat
Was so conspicuously
Set among all the other seats in arrangement
With distinct recognition in enchantment
Guests came in ...
More guests came in ...
No one went to sit on it
Despite the congestion
And smallness of room
I went to the host
And asked her in whisper...
I am a stranger here
and don't understand
Why no one goes to set on that vacant seat
She said quietly in a gentle voice...
"That who sits on that seat"
"His spirit will abandon him upon contact"
Upon hearing the answer
I thanked God
for not going to sit on that seat
on my own without knowing its horrific consequences

Rain the Drummer, Window the flutist...

The rain is pouring
Make music continuously
On the roof and from the gutter
Yes this is the sound of home
And this sound becomes ever more homey
As the rain keeps pouring for days

There ...
Learn to take care of your roof & gutter on time
To enjoy this primordial music non- stop
That touches your soul closer than
Your own bones
Without being interrupted by
Roof leaking and gutter overflowing
Those two untimely annoyances
Interfering with your music time relaxation

Water

My
Wife's
Name
Is Shiloh
In Persian means
The flame
But she loves water
Constancy
Jumping in pool in winter
And swimming in the sea in summer
How on earth
I can teach her jar that
One day she might
Get extinguished by
The love that
She is in love with

O

Human mind
Is made of
So many fine and finer path ways
Which allow for
Human sublime communication's
In form of delicate art forms
And what not
But there are visions and ideas
So sublime and so delicate
Beyond any human mind's reach for processing
No matter how delicate
The internal structure is woven & crafted
In order to sharing them
With the outside world
Communicably

Be Happy Now...

While alive
Don't
Worry
Too much
About where
You will be buried
After you die
For we all
Live a global village
And in this tiny village
No matter where you buried
You will be so close without a doubt
To your next kin village fellow human being

Even if your body
Is turned into
Dust and powder
Scattered around...

Just Don't Worry!

The Never Learn

He
has
climbed
the tallest seven mountains in the world
All the way to the top
yet upon his return
He is still expected to listen and obey those
who in their attempt
have failed to climb
even a smallest hill
in the vicinity
why?
As an acknowledgement that
He has not yet conquered
The tallest mountain ever
The summit of Mt. Heart in victory
To warrant him
The firing squad
To be used against
The disobedience

Swiftly: Gate of Aging Revealed

Transition
From youth
To elderly
Takes place
Through
A fine tunnel
That tunnel
Is nothing
But your own hair line
As it changes color
From what it used to be
To the gray one
To convince you
En route your vision that
It is time
To let the old person
Come inside
To reside in your soul
Instead of blocking it all out
At your door steps swiftly

In The Moment

Social revolution
Is like
An anticipated
Spontaneous
Hot sex
Out of blue
That has lasted
Only for a short intense while
But with bitter unfamiliar consequences
To face with
With no end in sight

It has happened before
It will happen again
And we will again regret it

That's for sure
We will never learn
I guarantee it

The Limits of Empire: The Trio

After
Passage of so many years
I went to visit
my local liquor store friend
but surprise! Surprise!
He had advanced and expanded
His humble one door shop
To a luxurious four door shop
He had even set aside a spot called
"Cheap Seat"
Where very inexpensive wines were piled up
For people with low budget
I congratulated him for his business success
And then I whispered into his ears saying:
You are not going to expand to Gabble up the next
door bakery
And then the next door cheese corner shop
Do you?
Because once gobbled up
Wine without cheese and bread is meaningless
in response he said
Body I watch my business greed in every step of the way
because I cannot imagine the world without the trio

When Birds Stop Singing

There were
Six electric cables
Going over my head
And the pagans that you could count them easily
Were sitting in there
The birds kept coming and going
Over my head
Each time a new music note
Was written by pagans on cables over there
The guitar orchestra went for hours
Created by birds could be overheard
What was the title of their music?
Yes, it was about being polite & courteous
when you are before your dad

Get Me Out of Here~

When
Man's life
Is safe and secure
Greed and envy
Rip through his soul
To push him to acquire
More wealth and greater properties
But when his life in an imminent danger
He is willing to give up everything
Including his underwear
To save his life
This only says
Man's psychic make up
Is made of two extreme and opposite poles of
proclivities
And with no happy medium in between

The Mercy in Hot Hell...

Put
the lobster
with head first
inside the boiling water
to mammons his pain and suffering
during the cooking...
And the lobster
gradually change color
From a pale brownish
To a vivid lovely live color
Somewhere between shiny red and orange
What is the subliminal message
Relayed by the Lobster in the boiling water?

Oh the Holy Lord...
Make the boiling and fairy hell ever hot and hotter!

Long & Extended Shower

Dust off your room
Polish you mirror
Vic cu mm the carpet
Move the furniture around
To clean the settled spider web
Hiding there as permanent resident
Shine the windows
Change the mattress and pillow cover
With fresh one
Sanitize the surrounding with spray
Let the fresh air blow in
When all is done
You feel as if
You have been baptized freshly clean
In bath tub for hours
Insulated from all the sins around you
There...
The more cleaning & cleansing you do in details
the more sinless you become

Become Water...

Man
By nature
Striving with teeth and nail
To go up and climb up more
In the social pyramid of society
Yet hardly noticing the water lesson
That constantly descend and descend more
Until it reaches the magnificent ocean
Some even go way down deeper
To make the underground water reservoir

The river in all dancing
The river in all bouncing
The river in all twisting
The river in all curving
The river in all flip flapping
Always heading down
Rolling...

Life Stages

Man in life
Goes through a series of life stages
Just in the same manner
The caterpillar
Passes through several stages
Until it becomes butterfly
Ready to lay legs
Thus each stage grows into a
Comfortable cozy cocoon one
Before moving into the next
And those men who hesitate
To leave the cocoon on time
By digging a hole in it for escape
Are doomed to be burned alive
In hot boiling water from beyond
Rendering his life mission unaccomplished
Unable to ascend to his next life stage
You have got way comfortable?
This is a warning sign my friend!
Get out at once!

The Ocean Mill: Humbling the Rocks

Large rocks...
Smaller rocks...
Rounded stones...
Smaller stones...
Petite marbles...
Now sands ...
As smooth as Chinese silk
But they are all
The procession of
Large to smaller to finer ones in parade
Right before yours eyes
In the grinding machinery of ocean
mill
That has taken the time of eternity
To perform the task
In split second in condensation
For your viewing

The Roots of Autumn

The season of fall
Has stripped the tall stark trees
From all their leaves
Turning it into a complete naked one
Now after the undressing
The tree looks like
And inverted one in upsetting
With all the underground roots exposed
But this time facing the heaven
With head got stuck in the dark underworld
In complete invisibility

The Stone Intelligentsia

Nothing
Bugs
an accomplished
Famous pride intellectual
than to take him
to the graveyard
showing him
His final destiny
with all the books
He has written piled up under his arms
and the medallions
He has been decorated with
now put in the safe lock box

Bed Time Praying: 08

Now
That
I am
Entering
Into the new world of sleep
For several hours
Let me have good dreams
Instead of bad ones
Like a drunken man
Who wish to have an all night joy partying
When his world has been transformed suddenly
From the solid
To that of vapor one without boundary

Musical Improvisation

Each leaf
On the tree
Is a string
Is a keyboard
And when the wind blows into the trees
In twist and curve and in rattle
It will make music
With zillions and trillions of leaf notes
All played out in the vast forest platform
Now the autumn has arrived
And the wind has no choice but to improvise
By using trees' trunk and remaining fine and finer
branches
As string tool for the music to play
Before the inhabitants of earth

Joy! And Only Joy! Period!

This moon
How many grand human gathering has witnessed
This moon
How many long wars has observed Being waged
amongst men
This moon
How many human catastrophe on earth has gazed at
This moon
How many prophets & preachers has seen who have
come and gone
Surely this moon
Has witnessed quite a lot
Despite his youth and his inexperience
And despite the old age experienced human inhibition
on earth
Therefore let's have a round of applause
For this novice moon
Before we get back to our own tiresome &
Everlasting & grown up business of society

Still

It
Is
Time
Now
To
Let
God
Reign....
And
You
Know
What
I
Am
Speaking of
or
You
Don't
Still

So

Far
I have not
Seen a leaf
In my whole life
Without full symmetry
Except when some of them
Have here and there a hole
On their thin and fragile 'n delicate bodies
When in the season of autumn
Began diving downward
In dance for earth
To utter out loud:
The Perfection
In absolute
At the end
Belongs
To thy
God
O
N
L
Y
A
N
D
O
N
L
Y

Oh Wind Blow Me Away Farther...

It
is autumn
and leaves
Separating from mother tree
in death dance
to fly away as far as they can
from their mother
before landing
to declare their freedom
and distance from crowd & congestion

we are all dying for freedom!

Transformation: The Heavenly Birds

I have hung
A bird feeder
Outside of my room
And intermittently
Here comes this and that bird in boom
During their comfortable feast
On the bird feeder out in Rome
I watch them with my binoculars
While sitting comfortable in my own dome
Now the birds are eating from the bird feeder
Right inside my room
As if their bodies have been transformed into light
To cross so easy the glass window come to my room
Oh the birds are all in my room
Without mess and germs or droppings
While singing and eating free all in my room

The Dexterity

Toward a Flexible World

Left hand is the eastern hemisphere
The right hand the western one
I gently bring these two half world near each other
Until each finger touches its corresponding
counterpart
Now I can see the entire rounded planet earth
Formed from my ten fingers
With five windows
Corresponding to five continents exist in earth
Corresponding to five oceans of earth
To make this rounded fingers planet earth complete
Bend the fingers inward and outward
At their point of convergence a bit
Now you see five windows of love opened up on earth
Each after the image of man's heart

The rounded flexible earth
Like the man's beating heart

Body Dimension

I
Am
Body
Do not cross me
For then be one without food
I
Am
Wine
Do not cross me
For you then be one
Without drink and water

Do not cross me...

Give the Outside World a Chance to Speak

Your
Brain
May work
Like a car ingénue
Without interruption
In constant creation of new idea
But it would be unwise
If you don't turn it all off for a while
To let the outside world
Begins to pour its own idea & signs
Into your head
Like a waterfall
Joining the ocean in an astounding sound with a new
message

"Fight Kais"

Yes
With only several gallons of water
Along with a hidden water pump
Coupled with all its well camouflaged tubes
You can make a waterfall
That can make soothing sound until eternity
As long as
You can pay the electric bill
With foundation leak free
You want to see a more fancy one
Then let's go Los Vegas
To see Bella Io spectacular water show
When time comes for family vacation
After some hard work done

The Ocean Cow

The ocean
Has brought
Tons of sea weeds and other greenery
On the shore
And then let it all rot and break down
Outside of the sea under the sun
When the time is ready for full digestion
To ocean takes back the regurgitated greenery
Back in his Tommy from the shore to his mouth
Surely the ocean is the cow
Chewing her food twice
Once in hurry
Second in slow motion and gentle
Laying down in comfort under sun
And then right back to his deeper belly'
From his shore mouth

Water Proof Shingles: Revisiting the Underwater Human Civilization

Most American homes' exterior
Is covered from head to toe
By layers of shingles
Row after row
Just like the fish scales
Not just to protect the body of house
From the beating of sun rays and rain storm
But to remind everyone that
The Atlantic civilization inside the ocean
Unlike the popular belief
Is safe and sound and well
With indisputable evidence of
School of fish in standstill
Scattered...
In diverse form of neighborhoods

Leaf is a poetic inspirational take on rebirth and resurrection of life on earth. Its theme is imaginary but with roots in reality of the industructibility of life in the midst of all lies.

Other Books from the Same Author

1. Rural Exodus & Squatter Settlements in the Third World. 1987. University Press of America

2. The Informal Economy: A Research Guide. 1991. Garland Press

3. Corridor of Hope: A Visual View of Informal Economy. 1999. University Press of America

4. Stars Light. First Volume. 2004. The AuthorHouse

5. Stars Light: Second Volume: Flame of Life. 2006. Airleaf Press

6. Stars Light: Third Volume: The Evening Dew. 2008. Mountain Valley Publishing Company

7. Stars Light: Fourth Volume: Sheida: Love Must Be Loved. 2008. Xlibris Publishing Company

Abol Danesh with a Ph.D. in sociology from university of California, picked up professorial position in sociology full time first in 1985 at Colby College in Maine for four years and then at the University of Rhode Island. He earned his professorship tenure in 1992. Danesh publisehd three volumes of his sociological research program during 1987-1999.

Later on, Danesh picked up poetry as an adjunct activity to his professorial career and published the first volume of Stars Light in 2004. His second volume of stars light appeared in 2006 under the rubric of Flame of Life. In 2008, Danesh published the third volume of stars entitled The Evening Dew. In the same year, his fourth volume emerged with the title of Love Must Be Loved. This fifth volume of stars with the title of leaf is an inspirational and healing work on the theme of resurrection and rebirth.

Danesh has been diagnosed with bipolar disorder and manic depression and have been struggling with this consuming disease since 2000. Gardening, long distance Walking, poetry writing, house cleaning, short distance running, bird watching are some of the things Danesh does to allievate the gripping pain of this illness over his soul and his spirit.

In the United States Danesh has lived in Texas, Maine, Rhode Island, and California.